NATIONAL GEOGRAPHIC

Explore the Midwest

Peter and Connie Roop

PICTURE CREDITS

Cover © Annie Griffiths Belt/Corbis; title page © Jim Richardson/National Geographic Image Collection; pages 2-3, 6-7, 13 (left), 25 (top right), 30 (top left), 31 (center right), 31 (bottom right), 34-b, 34-e © Tom Bean/Corbis; pages 4, 5, 25 (top left), 35-b illustrations by Rose Zgodzinski; pages 8 (top), 26 (bottom), 31 (top left), 31 (bottom left), 36 © Corbis; page 8-15 (background) © Darrell Gulin/Corbis; pages 8 (bottom), 35-f © Age Fotostock/SuperStock; page 9 © James L. Amos/Corbis; pages 10, 31 (top right) © Robert Holmes/Corbis; pages 11, 31 (center left), 35-d © Fred Hultstrand History in Pictures Collection, NDIRS-NDSU, Fargo; page 12 (left) © Geoffrey Clifford/Getty Images; page 12 (right) © Richard Olsenius/National Geographic Image Collection; pages 13 (right), 25 (bottom left), 34-f © Joe Scherschel/National Geographic Image Collection; page 14 (left) © Glen Allison/Getty Images; page 14 (right) © Craig Aurness/Corbis; pages 15, 34-a © Journal-Courier/Steve Warmowski/The Image Works; pages 16-17, 25 (bottom right), 35-c © Alan Schein Photography/Corbis; page 18 (top) © The Granger Collection; pages 18-23 (bottom borders) © Frank Cezus/Getty Images; page 19 (center) © The Bridgeman Art Library; page 20 (top) © Stock Montage; page 21 (top) © Bettmann/Corbis; page 22 (top) © Joseph Sohm/Corbis; pages 23 (center), 34-c © Russell Gordon/Odyssey Productions, Inc.; page 26 (top) © John Coletti/Index Stock; page 27 © Paul Damien/Getty Images; page 28 (top) © Layne Kennedy/Corbis; page 28 (bottom) © Steve Skjold/Photo Edit; page 29 © Ryan/Beyer/Getty Images; page 30 (top right) © James Leynse/Corbis; page 30 (bottom left) © Archive Holdings/Getty Images; page 30 (bottom right) © Chet Gordon/The Image Works; page 32 Getty Images; page 33 (left) *The Midwest* by Elspeth Leacock © 2002 National Geographic Society, photo © Paul Chesley/Stone/Getty Images; page 33 (center) *The Midwest: Its History and People* by Kate Connell © 2003 National Geographic Society, photos (top) © Smithsonian American Art Museum/Art Resource, NY, (bottom) © Tony Stone/Getty Images; page 33 (right) *The Midwest Today* © 2004 National Geographic Society, photo © Bill Ross/Corbis; page 34-d © David R. Frazier Photolibrary, Inc.; page 35-a © Jan Butchofsky-Houser/Corbis; page 35-e © The Detroit Institute of Arts/The Bridgeman Art Library.

Produced through the worldwide resources of the National Geographic Society, John M. Fahey, Jr., President and Chief Executive Officer; Gilbert M. Grosvenor, Chairman of the Board; Nina D. Hoffman, Executive Vice President and President, Books and Education Publishing Group.

PREPARED BY NATIONAL GEOGRAPHIC SCHOOL PUBLISHING

Ericka Markman, Senior Vice President and President, Children's Books and Education Publishing Group; Steve Mico, Senior Vice President, Editorial Director, Publisher; Francis Downey, Executive Editor; Richard Easby, Editorial Manager; Anne Stone, Lori Dibble Collins, Editors; Bea Jackson, Director of Layout and Design; Jim Hiscott, Design Manager; Cynthia Olson, Art Director; Margaret Sidlosky, Illustrations Director; Matt Wascavage, Manager of Publishing Services; Sean Philpotts, Production Manager; Ted Tucker, Production Specialist.

MANUFACTURING AND QUALITY CONTROL

Christopher A. Liedel, Chief Financial Officer; Phillip L. Schlosser, Director; Clifton M. Brown III, Manager

◀ A man canoes on one of the Midwest's many lakes.

Contents

CONSULTANT AND REVIEWER
Mark H. Bockenhauer, Ph.D., Associate Professor of Geography, St. Norbert College, De Pere, Wisconsin

BOOK DESIGN/PHOTO RESEARCH
Steve Curtis Design, Inc.

Published by the National Geographic Society
1145 17th Street N.W.
Washington, D.C. 20036-4688

ISBN: 0-7922-5458-9

2010 2009 2008
3 4 5 6 7 8 9 10 11 12 13 14 15

Printed in Canada.

Build **Background**

Five Regions

The United States is a large country. It has 50 states. These states can be broken into five **regions,** or groups. The five regions are the Northeast, the Southeast, the Midwest, the Southwest, and the West.

A region is an area, such as a group of states, with something in common. Each region has its own history and kinds of land. Each region has its own **culture,** or way of life. In this book, you will read about the Midwest region.

region – an area, such as a group of states, with something in common

culture – a way of life

CANADA
N
W
E
S
Lake Superior
MINNESOTA
WISCONSIN
Lake Michigan
Lake Huron
Mississippi River
MICHIGAN
Milwaukee
Detroit
Lake Erie
Chicago
IOWA
Cleveland
OHIO
ILLINOIS
INDIANA
MISSOURI
St. Louis
KANSAS

1 Understand the **Big Idea**

Welcome

Big Idea
The Midwest is shaped by its geography, history, economy, and people.

Set Purpose
Read to learn about life in the Midwest.

The Midwest region is in the middle of the United States. There are 12 states in the Midwest. These states stretch from Ohio to North Dakota and Kansas. Across the Midwest, you will find farms, factories, and cities. The Great Lakes and the Mississippi River are here, too. What else does the Midwest have?

Questions You Will Explore

What is the Midwest known for?

How has the land shaped the economy of the Midwest?

to the Midwest

A machine harvests wheat from a field.

▲ This stretch of water connects two of the Great Lakes.

▲ Ships such as this carry goods on the Great Lakes.

The Great Lakes

Four of the five Great Lakes are in the Midwest. They are Lake Superior, Lake Michigan, Lake Huron, and Lake Erie. They are called "Great Lakes" because they are so large. Lake Superior is the biggest. It is the largest freshwater lake in the world.

The Great Lakes are important to the Midwest. Large ships **transport** goods on the Great Lakes. Many people visit the Great Lakes. They come to swim, fish, and boat.

transport – to move

▲ **Cranes rest at a water source on the Great Plains.**

The Great Plains

Much of the Midwest is flat. The flattest part of the Midwest is called the Great Plains. These plains start near the Mississippi River. They stretch west to the Rocky Mountains.

The Great Plains were once covered with tall grass. Many animals, such as buffalo, lived on the grassy plains. Today, big farms cover the Great Plains. Farmers grow corn and wheat in the rich soil. The plains are still home to all kinds of animals. Many birds fly across the Great Plains in the spring and fall.

▲ **Native Americans hunted buffalo for meat and skins.**

Native Americans

Long ago, herds of buffalo lived on the Great Plains. The buffalo grew fat on the tall grass that grew there. Native Americans hunted the buffalo. They ate buffalo meat. Native Americans used buffalo skins to make clothes. They also used the skins to make their homes. These buffalo-skin homes were called **tepees.**

tepee – a tent used by Native Americans

▲ **Pioneer families once lived in houses like this, made of sod.**

Pioneers

Thousands of people moved to the Great Plains in the 1800s. These people were called **pioneers.** They came from the East to farm the Great Plains.

There are few trees on the Great Plains. So pioneers built their houses out of blocks of **sod.** Sod is a thick top layer of soil. Strong roots held the sod together. Grass and flowers grew out of sod houses!

pioneer – an early settler

sod – a thick top layer of soil

Parts of the Farm Belt

wheat

corn

Farming

Part of the Midwest is called the **Farm Belt.** The soil here is good. There are many farms and farmers. The Farm Belt has three main parts.

- The Wheat Belt grows lots of wheat.
- The Corn Belt grows lots of corn.
- The **Dairy** Belt makes lots of milk, butter, and cheese.

Farmers in the Farm Belt grow many other crops, too. Midwest farmers feed many people around the world.

Farm Belt – the part of the Midwest that has many farms

dairy – having to do with milk, butter, or cheese

▲ A worker makes steel for bridges, buildings, and cars.

Manufacturing

Part of the Midwest is called the Manufacturing Belt. **Manufacturing** is the making of things. Many people in the Midwest work in **factories.** They make steel, cars, and other products.

Some cities are known for manufacturing. For example, Detroit is known for making cars. Some people call Detroit the "Motor City." St. Louis and Cleveland have many factories. Milwaukee and Chicago do, too.

manufacturing – the making of things

factory – a place where products are made with machines

The city of St. Louis is in Missouri.

This small farming town is in Iowa.

Living in the Midwest

The Midwest has big cities like St. Louis. It has farms and small towns, too. In cities, people work in stores, banks, and offices. They have jobs in manufacturing. In small towns, many people have jobs that help farmers. They fix machines. They sell farm supplies and equipment. Farming is important to the Midwest.

▲ People enjoy the rides and games at a county fair.

A Special Region

The Midwest is a special region. Its culture is shaped by the things that are made here. The crops that are grown here are important, too.

Every summer and fall, the Midwest holds county fairs. These fairs have rides and games. They have displays and competitions, too. Fairs celebrate the hard work for which the region is known.

Stop and Think!

What is life like in the Midwest?

2 Take a **Closer Look**

Recap

Describe what life is like in the Midwest.

Set Purpose

Read to learn more about one big midwestern city, Chicago.

▼ **Many buildings in Chicago face Lake Michigan.**

Chicago

City by the Lake

Many people live on farms and in small towns in the Midwest. But there are many big cities, as well. Chicago is the biggest city in the Midwest. Chicago is the third biggest city in the United States. A long time ago, Chicago was just one log cabin. Today, millions of people live, work, and play here.

▲ **Fort Dearborn was built near Lake Michigan.**

It Started With a Cabin

Jean du Sable was a trader. He traded with Native Americans near Lake Michigan. Over 200 years ago, he built a cabin near the lake.

In 1803, people built a fort near Du Sable's cabin. The fort was called Fort Dearborn. Soon more traders came. A village grew. The traders named their village Chicago.

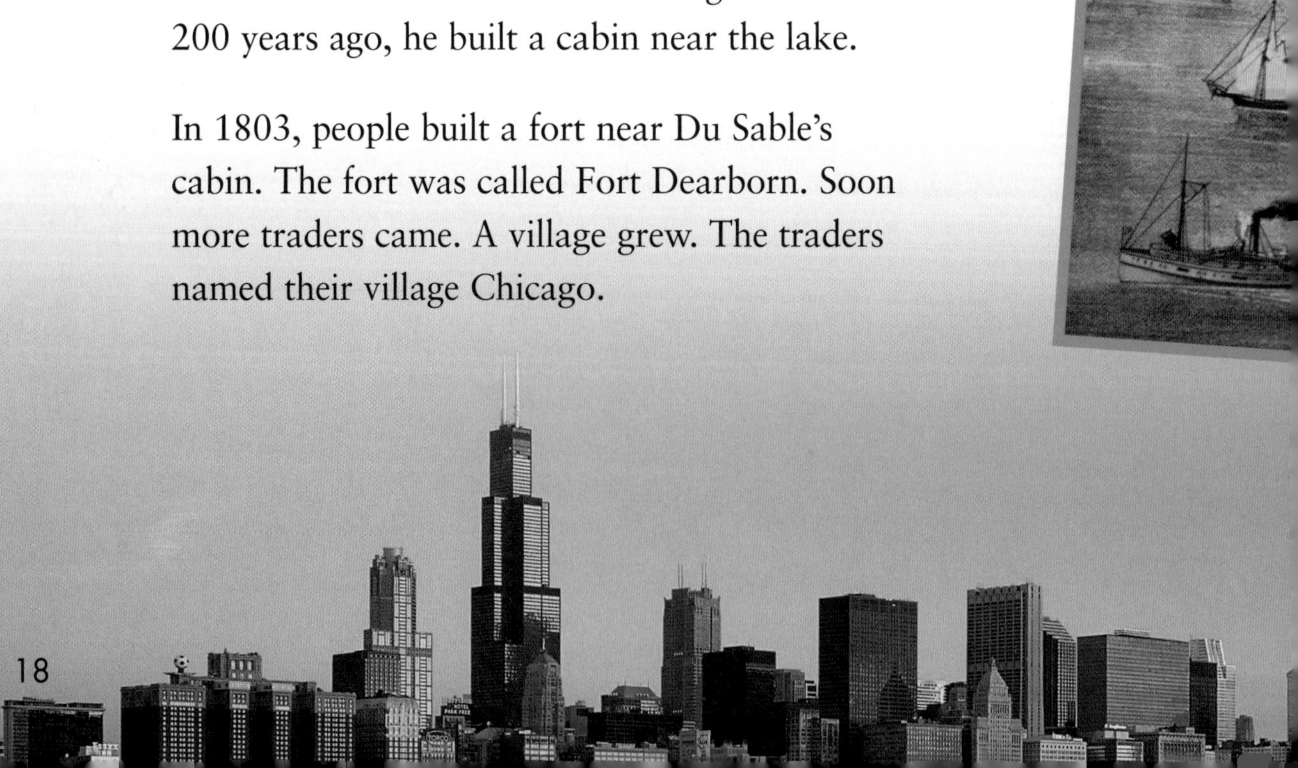

Chicago Grows

Chicago was easy to get to, so many people moved here. Some people came in ships and canoes. Others rode horses or came on foot.

By 1837, Chicago was growing fast. It had hundreds of stores, factories, and homes. Railroads came to Chicago in the 1850s. Trains brought more people to live and work in the city.

▼ **Chicago grew from a small village into a large city.**

▲ A fire destroyed most of Chicago in 1871.

Fire!

For a time, most buildings in Chicago were made of wood. Some streets were even paved with wood! One day in 1871, a small fire started in the city. The weather was dry. The wooden buildings were dry. Soon, almost all of Chicago was on fire. Thousands of people lost their homes. More than 300 people lost their lives.

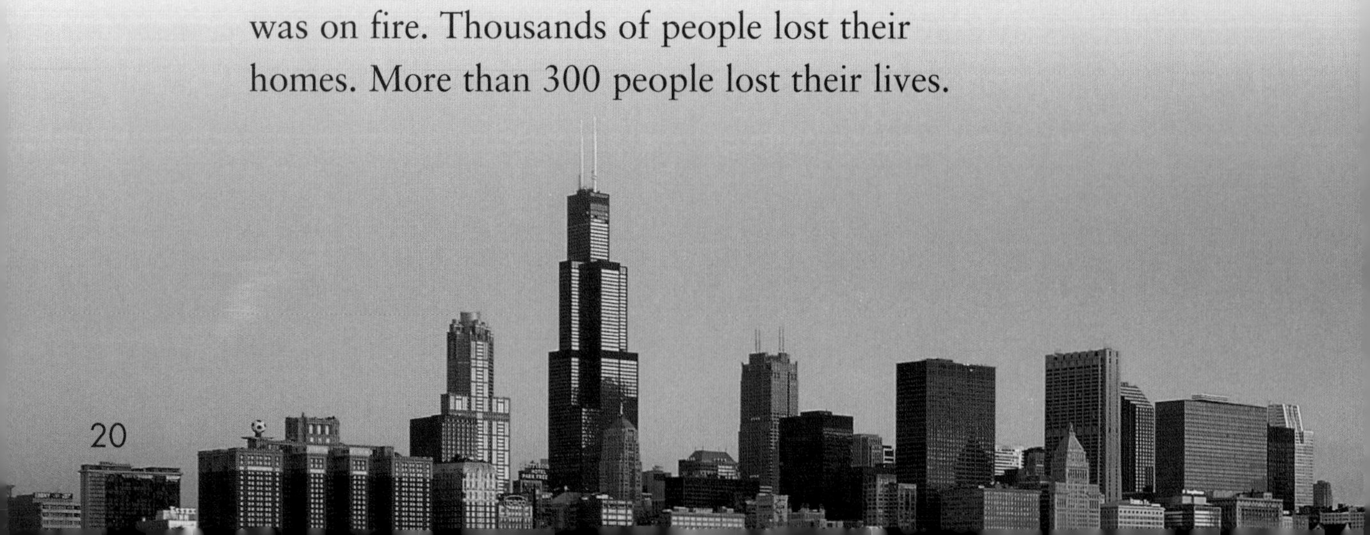

A New Chicago

Some people thought Chicago would not be rebuilt. They were wrong. Before long, new buildings were built. This time people used bricks and stone instead of wood. Some buildings were built out of steel. These buildings could be very tall. People called them **skyscrapers.** They seemed to touch the sky.

skyscraper – a very tall building

▼ **Chicago built bigger, stronger buildings after the fire.**

▲ **Chicago is now a busy city.**

Chicago Today

Chicago has grown from a small trading fort. It is now the third largest city in the country. Lake Michigan has helped Chicago grow. The lake means that goods can reach Chicago by ship. Goods can also come by plane, truck, and train. Chicago is a busy city. Its airport is one of the busiest in the world.

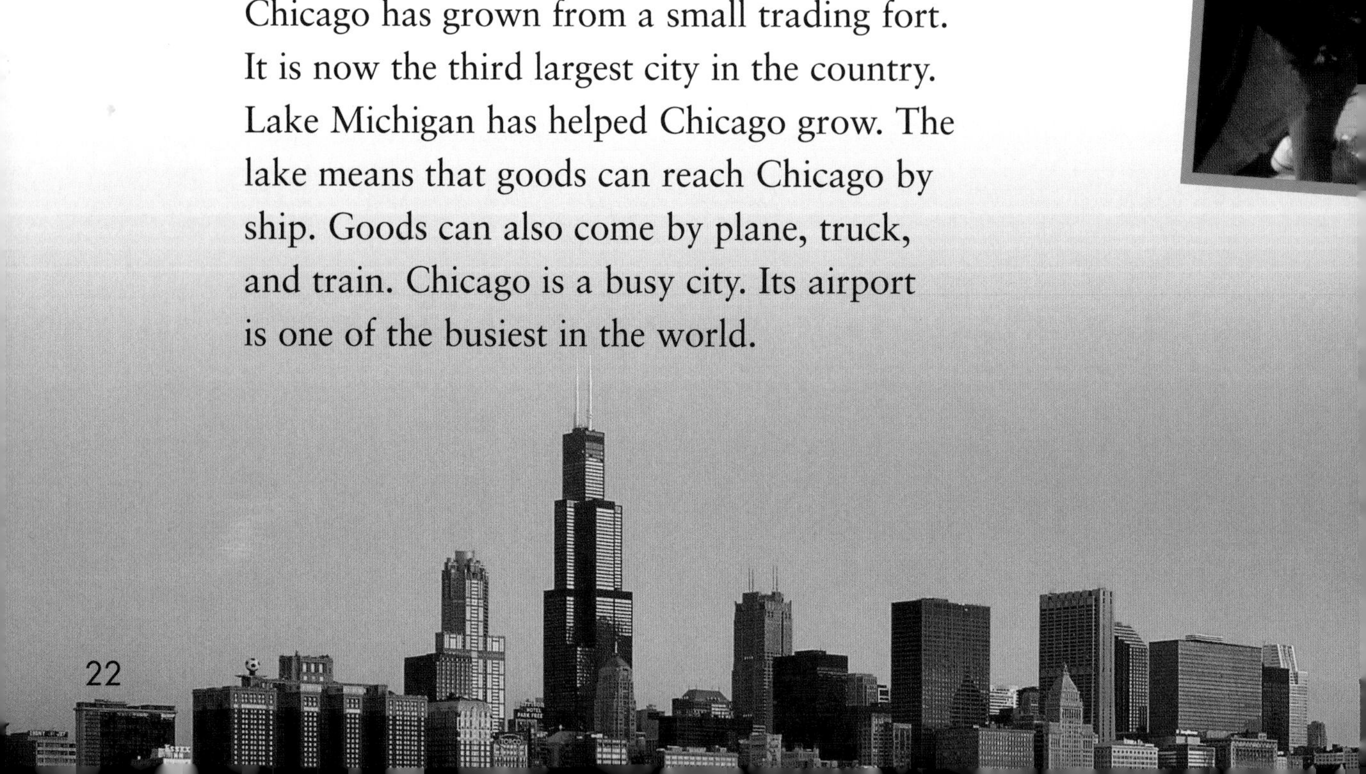

Many Neighborhoods

People from all over the world live in Chicago. Many people live in **ethnic** neighborhoods. For example, Chicago has Italian neighborhoods. It also has Polish neighborhoods. It has a Chinatown, too. Each neighborhood has its own culture. This is one reason Chicago is a special place to live, work, and play.

ethnic – having to do with people who have the same culture

▲ **An ethnic festival in Chicago**

Stop and Think!

Why did Chicago become such an important city?

Recap
Tell what makes Chicago a special city.

Set Purpose
Read to learn more about the Midwest.

CONNECT WHAT YOU HAVE LEARNED

Explore the Midwest

The Midwest is a large region in the middle of the country. It has big cities, small towns, and many farms.

Here are some ideas that you learned about the Midwest.

- The Midwest stretches from Ohio to North Dakota and Kansas.
- There are many farms in the Midwest because the soil is rich.
- Factories in the Midwest make steel, cars, and many other goods.
- The Midwest has the Great Plains and Great Lakes. It has big cities, too.

Check What You Have Learned

HOW is the Midwest shaped by its land, history, economy, and people?

▲ **The Midwest has 12 states and four of the five Great Lakes.**

▲ **Farming is an important part of the Midwest economy.**

▲ **Manufacturing is also a big part of the economy.**

▲ **Chicago is the biggest city in the Midwest.**

Faces in Stone

The Midwest is famous for two rock sculptures. One is Mount Rushmore National Memorial. This is one of the biggest stone carvings in the world. The faces of four presidents are carved into Mount Rushmore. The presidents are George Washington, Thomas Jefferson, Teddy Roosevelt, and Abe Lincoln.

The Crazy Horse Memorial is another big rock carving. Crazy Horse was a famous Native American. His carving is not yet done. When it is finished, it will be bigger than Mount Rushmore!

◀ **The Crazy Horse Memorial**

◀ **A tornado twists and spins across a field.**

▼ Mount Rushmore National Memorial

CONNECT TO WEATHER

Tornado!

There are over 1,000 tornadoes every year in the United States. A tornado is a special kind of storm. The wind blows very hard. It spins very fast. The strong winds make a tornado sound like a train!

The Midwest is famous for its many tornadoes. Some tornadoes do only a little damage. Others destroy homes, schools, and stores. People in the Midwest take cover when a tornado comes.

▲ A worker slices cheese into blocks.

Cheeseheads

Wisconsin is famous for cheese. Wisconsin makes more cheese than any other state. It makes over 350 different kinds of cheese.

People in Wisconsin have been making cheese for more than 150 years. They are proud of their many kinds of cheese. Some people wear foam hats shaped like a piece of cheese. People call them cheeseheads!

▶ Wisconsin cheeseheads

The Mississippi River

The Mississippi River runs through the Midwest. It is one of the longest rivers in the United States. It flows from Minnesota south to the Gulf of Mexico.

The Mississippi is a very busy river. Barges carry heavy loads up and down the river. People use the Mississippi River for fun, too. They swim, fish, and boat on the mighty Mississippi.

▼ The Mississippi River starts in Minnesota.

Zoom in on Words

Many kinds of words are used in this book. Here you will learn about words that have more than one meaning. You will also learn about words that describe a person, place, or thing.

Multiple-Meaning Words

Some words have more than one meaning. Think about the two meanings for each of these words. Then use each word in a sentence of your own.

The Wheat **Belt** produces wheat for bread and cereal.

This man likes to wear a **belt.**

The **train** brought people to live and work in Chicago.

Athletes **train** hard for their sporting events.

Adjectives

An adjective is a word that describes a person, place, or thing. An adjective often goes before the word it describes. Which words do the adjectives describe below?

The Midwest has many **special** areas, such as the Great Lakes.

Native Americans used **buffalo** skins to make their homes.

Pioneers built **sod** houses.

Cows on a **dairy** farm produce milk for butter and cheese.

The **rich** soil in the Farm Belt is good for crops.

Much of the land in the Midwest is **flat.**

Research and Write

Write About the Midwest

You read about the Midwest region. Now learn more about how its farmers help the rest of the country. Research life on a midwestern farm. Then write a report telling what you have learned.

Research
Collect books and reference materials, or go online.

Read and Take Notes
As you read, take notes and draw pictures.

Write
Now write a paragraph describing the kind of farm you chose. What products does the farmer sell? Who uses these products? Why are the products important?

Read and Compare

Read More About the Midwest

Find and read other books about the Midwest. As you read, think about these questions.

- What influences have shaped this region?
- What makes this region special?
- How is this region important to the rest of the country?

Books to Read

▲ **Take a guided tour through the states of the Midwest.**

▲ **Find out about the events and people that helped build the Midwest.**

▲ **Learn more about the culture and contributions of the Midwest.**

Glossary

KEY CONCEPT

culture (page 4)
A way of life
County fairs are part of the culture in the Midwest.

KEY CONCEPT

dairy (page 12)
Having to do with milk, butter, or cheese
There are many dairy farms in the Midwest.

ethnic (page 23)
Having to do with people who have the same culture
Chicago has many ethnic neighborhoods.

factory (page 13)
A place where products are made with machines
Detroit has many factories that make cars.

KEY CONCEPT

Farm Belt (page 12)
The part of the Midwest that has many farms
Farmers in the Farm Belt grow wheat and other crops.

KEY CONCEPT

manufacturing (page 13)
The making of things
The Midwest is known for manufacturing.

pioneer (page 11)
An early settler
Thousands of pioneers moved to the Great Plains in the 1800s.

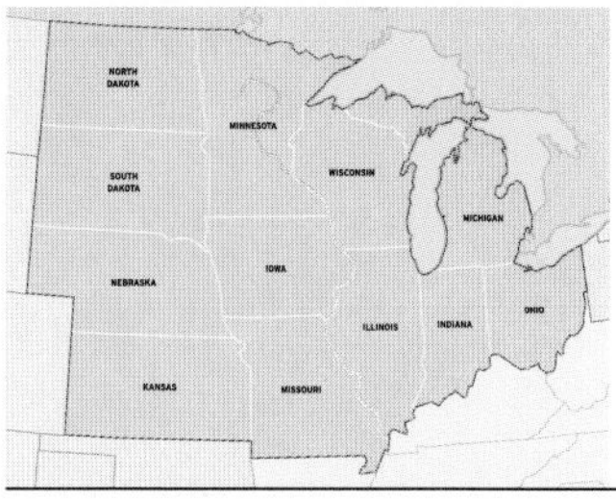

KEY CONCEPT

region (page 4)
An area, such as a group of states, with something in common
The Midwest is one of five regions in the United States.

skyscraper (page 21)
A very tall building
There are many skyscrapers in Chicago.

sod (page 11)
A thick top layer of soil
Pioneers built their homes out of blocks of sod.

tepee (page 10)
A tent used by Native Americans
Homes made out of buffalo skins were called tepees.

KEY CONCEPT

transport (page 8)
To move
Large ships transport goods on the Great Lakes.

Index